The EARTH

SCIENCE
UP
CLOSE

JULIAN MESSNER

Science Photo Library

PHOTO CREDITS

Jack Finch p. 3; NASA p. 4, 5, 6; Robin Scagell p. 7; Sinclair Stammers pp. 7, 14, 19(T.), 21; Michael Marten p. 8(T.); David Parker p. 8(B.); Nelson Medina p. 9; Claude Nuridsany and Marie Perennou p. 10(T.); James Stevenson p. 10(B.); Adam Hart-Davis pp. 11(T.), 30; Doug Allan p. 11(B.); Per Gloersen/Polar Record p. 12; P. Menzel p. 13(T.); R. Legeckis p. 13(B.); Martin Dohrn p. 15; Aeroservice p. 16; Earth Satellite Corporation pp. 17, 19(B.) 31; Simon Fraser p. 18; David Parker pp. 20, 22, 23; Matthew Shipp p. 24; Doug Allan p. 25; Steve Gull/John Fielden/Alan Smith p. 26; Cambridge University Collection of Air Photography p. 28; Rodney Henson p. 29; Ron Reid p. 32.

 Published by Julian Messner, a division of Silver Burdett Press, Inc., Simon & Schuster, Inc., Prentice Hall Bldg., Englewood Cliffs, NJ 07632. JULIAN MESSNER and colophon are trademarks of Simon & Schuster, Inc.
Design by R Studio T. Manufactured in the United States of America.
Lib. ed. 10 9 8 7 6 5 4 3 2 1
Paper ed. 10 9 8 7 6 5 4 3 2 1

Library of Congress Cataloging-in-Publication Data

Cleeve, Roger.
[Beautiful earth]
The earth / by Roger Cleeve.
p. cm.—(Science up close)
Reprint. Originally published: Beautiful earth. 1st ed. Brighton, England: Young Library, c1988.
Summary: Text and photographs introduce the earth's physical features, weather patterns, and urban areas.
1. Earth—Juvenile literature. 2. Earth—Photographs from space—Juvenile literature. [1. Earth.] I. Title. II. Series.
QB631.4.C54 1990
ISBN 0-671-68626-7 ISBN 0-671-68629-1 (pbk.)
550—dc20 89-29195
CIP
AC

The aurora borealis, or northern lights, seen over spruce trees in Alaska. Subatomic particles from the sun cause the rays, bands, streamers and curtains that make up the display.

One day, you might stand on the moon and gaze up at Earth. If you do, it will look like this. The parts that look blue are those that are covered by water.

Through gaps in the swirling white clouds, you can see the whole continent of Africa. The Arabian Peninsula lies just above and to the right of it, at the top of the picture.

This is a short length of the Mississippi River. The photo was taken from an airplane about three miles above the ground. There are fields, roads, stands of trees, islands, and sandbanks. The colors are not those that you would ordinarily see. That is because the photograph was taken in infrared light instead of ordinary visible light. The infrared shows healthy vegetation in shades of pink, red, and red-brown, instead of green.

This is a hurricane photographed from roughly two miles above. From there, it looks like a beautiful white cloud. However, its power is enormous. A hurricane is a whirling storm between 60 and 90 miles across. The winds near its center move at speeds up to 150 miles per hour. A hurricane can travel at 50 miles per hour across the ground. It can tear down power lines and houses and even blow trains off their tracks.

The picture above was taken from a mountaintop 6,800 feet high, in the Canary Islands, off Africa. It shows a blanket of cloud about a half mile thick. The distance from the ground to the lowest cloud is much less than from the lowest cloud to the highest. Up above such clouds, it is sunny. Underneath, it is dark and gloomy, as in the picture below showing storm clouds pouring across mountains in western Ireland.

A rainbow, like the one on the left, has bands of many colors. This one shows red, orange, yellow, green, blue, indigo, and violet bands. In a rainbow, the sun's rays are bent and reflected by raindrops. We have all seen such rainbows, but have you ever seen a frostbow, like the one below? In a frostbow, the sun's light is bent and reflected by ice crystals in the air.

Above, beautiful bolts of lightning flash in a black sky. Several seconds later, there will be a frightening crash of thunder. What is taking place in such cases? Lightning is a release of huge amounts of electricity. It usually happens when large rainclouds are near each other. The thunder occurs because of a rushing movement of the heated air.

Snow is made up of water vapor that has frozen into crystals, like the one on the left. Every snow crystal has a different pattern. The brilliantly white trees you see opposite are covered by millions of these beautifully patterned crystals.

When dripping water freezes, it forms icicles, like those on the holly branch shown at left. When light passes through such icicles, they can be as beautiful as a rainbow.

The huge mass of ice in the picture to the right is an iceberg. It has broken away from a sheet of floating ice in the Antarctic. It will drift hundreds of miles north, into warmer waters, before it melts. As big as it looks, only about one-eighth of it is visible above the surface. The rest is under water.

The three space-satellite images on these pages are temperature maps. Different colors show areas of different temperature. The map above is of ice-covered Antarctica. All the ice is cold, but—as you can see—some parts of it are colder than others. The white, green, and blue regions in the center are the coldest of all. Pictures like this are used to study changes in the ice cap.

The satellite image at the top of the opposite page shows nearly all of North and South America. It records the temperatures, and also shows how damp the air is.

The picture at the lower right shows the surface temperature of the sea off the Middle Atlantic coast of the United States. The dark land area on the left is much warmer than the sea. The blue area shows cold sea water. The pink area shows the warm waters of the Gulf Stream. This "river in the sea" flows from the Gulf of Mexico northeastward across the Atlantic Ocean.

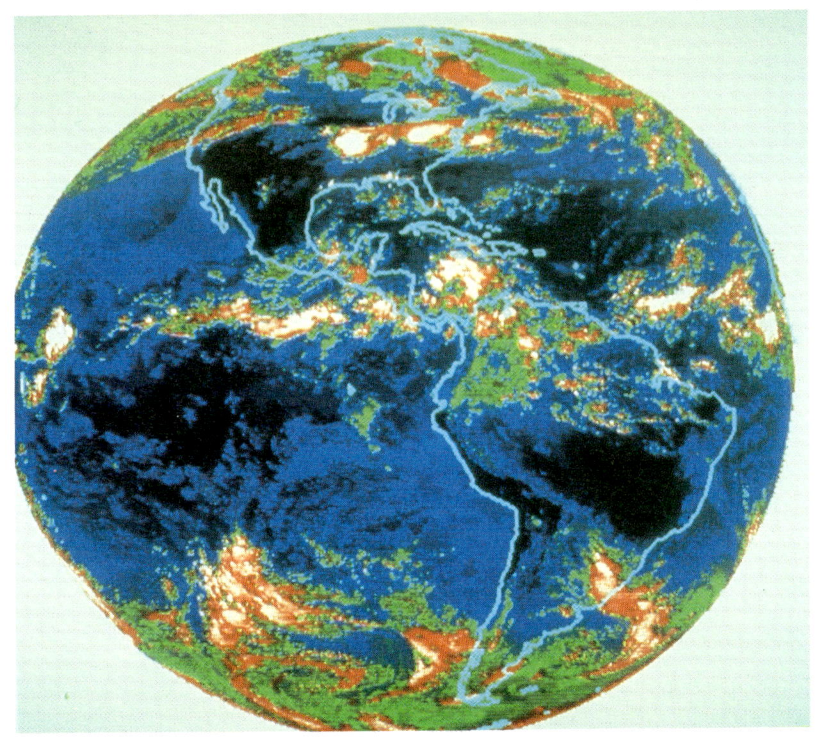

These cliffs on the coast of Wales in Great Britain are made up of many layers of rock. The layers slant now, but they were once level. Then, great movements far below ground caused the rock to sink downward in the middle. This process began about 400 million years ago and lasted about 40 million years.

Waves, like those shown opposite, do not usually arrive in a long, straight line. Their shape and length as they reach a beach are decided by the shape of the sea bed and the slope of the beach. In the picture, the surge of water pushes small rocks and sand toward land. Then it sucks them back again, to produce this zigzag pattern.

Before you read further, try to guess what the picture above shows. Is it a burning tree? Or an upside-down view of the roots of a bush reaching into the earth?

In fact, this is another photograph taken from high up in the sky. It shows the Colorado River delta in the Gulf of California. Here the river breaks up into many streams as it enters the sea. The black area is water, the blue is land, and the yellow shows sandbars.

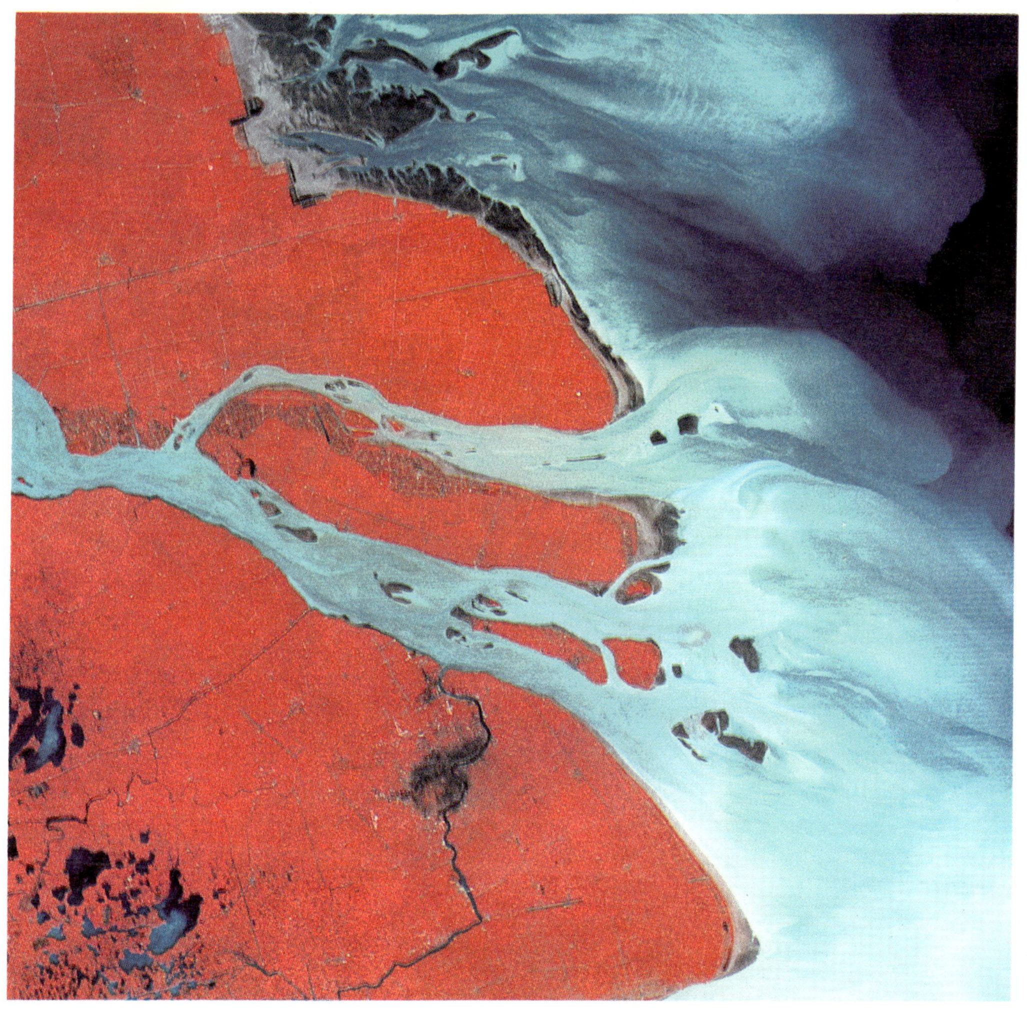

This picture is a satellite image of the Yangtze River delta on the coast of China. The sea is at the right in the picture. Inside the land area in the lower left, there are smaller rivers, lakes, and the straight lines of irrigation ditches. The gray smudge at the lower left is Shanghai, with its nearly 20 million people. The city is surrounded by vegetation, which looks red in the picture. The pale color of the Yangtze is caused by millions of tons of silt. The silt is soil carried out to sea from hundreds of miles inland. It created the islands you see in the picture.

The height of this huge mountain range in Kashmir, in Asia, rarely falls below 16,000 feet. At that height, the barren ice has an unshakable grip on the rock all year long. Despite its coldness, the area is a desert. It is very dry, and little can grow there.

The large picture opposite shows a very different kind of desert. It is a sandy desert. You can see the shifting dunes, or hills of windblown sand. Within days, the curving shapes of the dunes will be quite different.

The picture on the right is a satellite view of a hot and rocky desert. But what is the odd, claw-shaped pattern of red circles just below center? The circles are fields of crops irrigated, or watered, through long sprinkler pipes. Each pipe turns like the hand of a clock, throwing water in a circular pattern. The darker red circles show fully grown crops. The lighter red ones show early growth.

If you heat a chocolate mixture too long in a pan, the result might look like this. In fact, this is a picture of a drying river bed in Arizona. A few days before, water flowed along the river bed. But the water has trickled away, and now the sun sucks the last moisture out of the sticky mud.

The pattern on this page took much longer to form than the mud pattern opposite—about 180 million years. It shows the remains of creatures called ammonites. The ammonites had shells made up of many compartments. Each compartment formed as the ammonite outgrew the previous one. You are not actually looking at the shells themselves, but at their fossils. These fossils are the shapes left in the rock by the shells after millions of years.

The strange landscape opposite was created by water. In this valley in Utah, rain, snow, and melted ice drip constantly into cracks in the pink sandstone rock. About 200 times each year, the water freezes during the night and thaws again in the daytime. As it freezes, it expands, or swells, widening the cracks. After a few thousand years, the pressure splits the rock apart.

Time and water have also created arches, like the one above, in the Utah desert. Rain and wind batter the soft sandstone. Eventually, they wear a hole through the ridge. The hole grows bigger and bigger, until only the edges remain. The arch will last for a little while (a little while on the scale of the earth, that is—just a few million years). Then it will fall. By then, others will have been created.

This amazing burst of molten lava, or melted rock, is coming out of a volcano in Iceland. Our whole planet began as a mass of boiling melted rock. Over millions of years, the outer crust cooled down and turned solid. However, far below the surface, the rock is still in fiery, molten form. Occasionally, it breaks through in these fountains of lava and ash.

On the other side of the world, in New Zealand (opposite), the heat below ground creates a much gentler effect. Rainwater seeps through cracks to a great depth. There, it is heated by the rocks over which it passes. The metal-colored water then bubbles up through surface wells.

These four pictures show the earth at different times in its history. The continents did not always look the way they do today. That is because the earth is semiliquid deep inside. Great masses of the solid surface slide about on this molten inner part. They bump into each other or drift apart. Africa is still moving away from America at an average speed of almost an inch per year.

Make a drawing of how you think the continents will look after another 100 million years have passed. Perhaps you can use your school computer to help you figure out the likely shapes and positions.

50
million
years ago

0
million
years ago

If you stood in the bare English fields opposite, you would not be able to see the shadowy, zigzag lines shown near the center of the photo. They can be seen only from high above. They are caused by 2,000-year-old lanes and stone-filled ditches that now lie roughly 10 feet below the ground.

It is not possible to grow crops in the usual way on very steep slopes, such as those in Nepal shown above. Water and soil would slide to the bottom. Also, farm vehicles could not work well at steep angles. To solve this problem, farmers cut the hillside into low steps called terraces. Each step is level. When water overflows one terrace, it gently spills over to the next.

On these pages, you see two views of New York. The first shows a part of Manhattan Island. The photo was taken from the top of the Empire State Building, looking northeast. The skyscrapers look bent because they are seen through a "fish-eye" camera lens.

The larger picture is a satellite image. It also shows Manhattan, the long, narrow island that points upward (north) from the center of the photo, almost to its top edge. The Hudson River flows down along the left side of Manhattan. To the left of the river is New Jersey. Just below Manhattan is Brooklyn. Kennedy Airport, and the beginning of Long Island lie farther to the right. Gray-blue colors show built-up areas. Red shows grass or woods. What do you think the red patches in the built-up areas are?

This picture shows the sun setting over the ocean. Everything is changing color. Earlier in the day, the sky and sea were bright blue. Now the sky is turning orange, and the sea looks dark except where the sun's rays strike it. Soon night will fall. Sky and sea will look black, and the sun will be gone from the scene. But hours later, there will be light again, and the whole process will begin once more—another beautiful day on Planet Earth.